CHILDREN'S WILDLIFE GARDEN NOTEBOOK

⅍ The Oxford Illustrated Press

© 1984 Chris Baines
Printed in Great Britain by J. H. Haynes & Co Limited
ISBN 0 946609 17 9
The Oxford Illustrated Press,
Sparkford, Yeovil, Somerset

British Library Cataloguing in Publication Data

Baines, Chris
    Chris Baines' wildlife garden notebook.
    1. Wildlife habitat improvement
    2. Garden ecology
    I. Title
    639.9'2   SK355

ISBN 0-946609-17-9

Contents

Gardens for Wildlife

If you're like me, then I'm sure you will want your garden to be full of life. I love to hear birds singing, to see butterflies and bumblebees working away around the summer flowers, and to be able to enjoy primroses, bluebells and honeysuckle right on my doorstep. I want a little bit of countryside of my own. Modern gardening seems to have become a miniature version of high-technology farming, with lots of chemicals and machinery driving away the wildlife. With a little help, anyone can attract a wide variety of wild plants and animals back into their garden. Make a few simple changes, and in no time at all you will be sitting back and enjoying your own 'local nature reserve'. The wildlife that visits your garden will give you plenty of entertainment every month of the year, and you will have more time to enjoy it too, because with a rich-habitat wildlife garden there is less need for weeding, clipping, mowing and spraying. You will be working *with* nature, and that is bound to make life easier.

As a wildlife gardener, you will be helping to make a very important contribution to Nature Conservation. The wildlife in our countryside has suffered terribly in recent years. The combination of modern farming, building work around the edges of towns, new roads, forestry plantations and Dutch Elm disease has reduced the amount of wildlife habitat dramatically. We have destroyed more of our ancient woodlands in the past forty years than our ancestors managed to wipe out in the previous 400. Wildflowers such as the primrose and cowslip, which were quite common even thirty years ago, have become very rare indeed – mainly because their habitat has been destroyed. Of all the wildflower meadows that existed in 1949, over 95% have since been destroyed for ever. They have been built on, or ploughed, sprayed with herbicides, or simply fed with fertiliser to encourage more grass to grow. Losing all those wildflowers is bad enough, but of course as the meadows disappear, then we are also destroying the habitat for many of our butterflies and moths, our skylarks and all the other beautiful creatures which live there. It's high time we all started to *do* something.

With so much hostile pressure in the countryside, parks and gardens are obviously becoming more and more important for wildlife. There are 90% fewer frogs in some of the agricultural counties than there were ten years ago, but as ponds and ditches have been filled in or polluted in the farmland, there has been a boom in garden ponds. The population of frogs in towns has rocketed, and so private gardens have helped to save the day.

There are over a million acres of gardens in Britain. That is an enormous area of land, and if lots of people begin to provide a home for wildlife, then it is not hard to see how important this style of gardening can become. Of course gardens can't do very much to help the otter, or the osprey, or the red squirrel – they all need large areas of wild landscape, well away from people – but there are a great many native plants and animals that will be perfectly happy with a garden habitat.

Most of the larger, more spectacular garden animals need more territory than the average garden can provide. You may well have hedgehogs visiting you each evening through the summer, but they will probably be roaming over several of your neighbours' gardens, too. You may have dozens of birds feeding on the bird-table outside your kitchen window in January, but when the nesting season comes they will pair up and stake out their various territories and only one or two pairs will nest in your garden. In fact, many of them will fly thousands of miles north to Russia and Scandinavia before they eventually breed. As a wildlife gardener you need to take an interest in all the wild green spaces in your neighbourhood. If someone sprays the nettle-patch in the churchyard, or chops down the old trees in the parks, you will lose some of your wildlife visitors. Your success will be strictly limited if your garden has to operate as a self-contained island in a sea of tarmac and concrete.

As a first step towards wildlife gardening then, it is important to think of your garden as a 'service station' for passing wildlife. Try to develop ways of plugging into the wildlife corridor system of railway cuttings, canals and road verges. By providing plenty of undergrowth, lots of shelter and protection, and a regular supply of food, your garden will become more and more popular with the local birds, butterflies and other wandering beasties. Many of your visitors will come after dark, and you may not realise how busy your 'service station' gets, until you see the criss-cross pattern of tracks in the snow one winter's morning.

Most wildlife gardeners will already have a bird-table, and this is marvellous for attracting a whole variety of colourful birds, from blue tits to woodpeckers. You may also find the local grey squirrels moving in, and if they do your food bills will soar. Bird-tables are excellent, but limited. They really should be used only through the winter months, because baby birds can't digest foods like peanuts. They must have grubs. Some of the more secretive ground-feeding birds don't like using bird-tables very much at all. If you want to help them, it is well worth feeding on the ground. Choose a space well away from any bushes that might conceal a cat or two. Wrens, dunnocks, blackbirds, chaffinches and thrushes are all much happier down below.

In the summer you should forget about the 'fast-food' section of your service station, and concentrate on encouraging the insects. If the butterflies, beetles and hoverflies move into your patch, then the birds and mammals that feed on them will follow automatically.

The garden feature that will pull in most passing trade from the wildlife corridor system at this time of year is a colourful display of garden flowers. Masses of pollen and nectar will be irresistible to a whole host of beautiful insects. You should aim to provide a display for as long a period as possible. My garden opens with crocuses in February. These are followed by a procession of perfumed pollen plants such as wallflowers, polyanthus, honesty, petunias, tobacco-plants, sunflowers and autumn-flowering michaelmas daisies; in fact it's still going strong well into December with weary small tortoiseshell butterflies and a mass of different hoverflies feeding on the glistening droplets of nectar which cover the ivy flowers.

Many of the pollen and nectar plants help improve the garden habitat in other ways, too. Honesty for instance, has wonderful purple flowers in April and May, which attract a number of different species of spring butterflies. The leaves of honesty are also important for wildlife. The orange-tip butterfly lays its eggs on them, and the green caterpillars which eventually hatch out feed there happily for the rest of the summer -- unless, of course, they get snapped up to feed hungry baby blue tits. At the end of the summer, the honesty plants have formed big shiny white seedheads – these make a third contribution. As the cold weather sets in, bullfinches begin to visit the garden, and their favourite food in October and November seems to be honesty seed. The ivy climbing up the wall by my back door is another multi-purpose plant. The insects that enjoy its nectar in November are helping to pollinate the flowers. These produce big bunches of black fruit which become very important food for blackbirds, thrushes and pigeons, particularly in late winter, when most other fruits have run out. The ivy flowers are vital, too, for survival of the holly-blue butterfly. This pretty little insect lays its eggs there in October . The dense leaf cover makes my ivy a favourite place for wrens to nest, and in March the noisy little cock-wren flies in and out all day long, building one of a selection of nests for his mate to choose from. Several species of butterfly use the ivy as a safe place to hibernate, and one in particular, the brimstone, is perfectly camouflaged to look just like a dead ivy leaf. When it hangs itself up in the autumn it becomes almost impossible to see.

Not all plants are quite as useful as the ivy, of course, but certainly there are many garden flowers you might decide to grow because they produce useful seed in addition to their summer blossoms. The berries on cotoneasters, pyracantha and hawthorn, for example, will provide welcome food for the redwings and fieldfares when they arrive back from Russia to spend the winter here. Fallen apples are a favourite, and the fluffy seeds on the michaelmas daisies, the fat striped seeds of the 'dead' sunflower heads, the teasels, the marigolds and the giant thistles will all make your garden very popular through the autumn and winter if you leave them uncut. There really is no more colourful sight than a charm of goldfinches chattering to one another as they tease out the teasel seeds on a frosty December morning.

The final essential ingredient in any 'service station' wildlife garden is water. You will be surprised how much livelier the garden become – even if you only have room for a tiny 'puddle'. Many creatures will call in for a drink of course. You will get your fair share of the local cats and dogs, but you'll find that the wild birds and mammals in the area will visit your watering hole, too. Crowds of birds turn up to bathe around the edge of my pond, splashing away in the shallows throughout the year. I've seen as many as forty starlings, apparently enjoying themselves with a quick dip on a cold January morning. I can only assume that these are birds that spend their summers in northern Russia. I suppose that for them, my pond in January must be the equivalent of our holiday in the Mediterranean.

Of course ponds aren't just useful for drinking and bathing. There are many plants and animals that need water to survive and breed. Lots of our most colourful wildflowers live with their roots in marshy ground or underwater – plants like the flag iris, the ragged robin and the marsh marigold. The frogs I mentioned earlier, are disappearing from the countryside because their ponds are being filled in, and they have nowhere to mate and lay their frogspawn. Garden ponds are a vitally important habitat for all our amphibians – frogs, toads and newts. Dragonflies and damselflies, water boatmen, diving beetles, pond skaters and many more fascinating creatures cannot possibly survive unless we provide them with patches of unpolluted open water, and that leads me on to the other kind of wildlife gardening – habitat creation.

Service stations are all very well. They will allow you to see a wide range of wildlife at close quarters, but in a service-station wildlife garden you are really 'borrowing' the wildlife. You are dependent on the local park, the churchyard or the railway embankment to provide you with an endless supply of hungry visitors. Those visitors need much more than a drop-in snack – they need a place to live. That place could be your garden. Once you've established yourself as the most popular service station in the district, it is time to begin developing your 'Rich-Habitat Garden'.

Creating a Rich-Habitat Garden

Plants and animals are very choosy about where they live, and particularly about where they breed. If you want to create new habitats in your garden, to have wildflowers happily spreading and colonising, and to begin generating your own baby frogs, butterflies, songbirds and hedgehogs, then you must follow a few golden rules.

Rule 1: Grow some native plants

All native animal life depends on a supply of native plants. Even the most spectacular of meat-eating hunters, the owls, kestrels, stoats and foxes, all eat other smaller animals which themselves eat plants or other plant-eaters. The food chain begins with plants. Many of the grubs, caterpillars, aphids and other plant eaters are extremely specialised. They may well only be able to eat the leaves of one particular type of plant, and when this is the case, that plant will always be a native. Take the caterpillars of the small tortoiseshell butterfly for example. They can eat nothing except young leaves of stinging nettles. If you have small tortoiseshells dropping in to feed on your buddleia blossoms, or your michaelmas daisy flowers, they *must* have lived on a local nettle patch when they were caterpillars. The brimstone butterfly, a beautiful yellow insect, one of the first to emerge from hibernation on sunny April days, will fly for miles to find a bush of a plant called alder buckthorn, because that is one of only two native shrubs its caterpillars can eat. All native plants – trees, shrubs and wildflowers, will have their own dependent leaf-eating creepy-crawlies, and if you grow a range of plants you will attract a wider variety of insects. Hawthorn, for example, provides food for almost 150 different kinds. Pussy willow leaves are the essential food for well over a hundred more. Exotic plants like rhododendron, laurel or lilac rarely provide food for any species of insect larvae, but of course they may still be useful in offering a 'service station' supply of nectar or seed.

Rule 2: Allow room for decay

Gardens are generally far too tidy for wildlife. Many creatures need to hibernate through the cold winter. Some of the bigger ones – hedgehogs and woodmice for example – choose to curl up in piles of old leaves. Some of the 'mini-beasts' choose the hollow stems of dead flowers. Dead material is important as food for wildlife too. In fact, far more types of wild creatures feed on dead and rotting material than on living plants. Try not to clear away all the garden rubbish. If the lawn is covered with fallen leaves at the end of the summer, rake them up and throw them under the hedge, or at least compost them. It's a terrible waste just to burn them. A night-time visit with a torch, to take a peep at the compost heap, will quickly show you just how many creatures there are making a living out of the dead material in your rich habitat garden.

Rule 3: Cut down on chemicals

At the bottom end of the food chain, plant and animal life is very vulnerable. When the first greenfly appear in spring, it's always tempting to spray them with a chemical poison. Please don't! If you have just a little patience, you will see that a well-balanced rich-habitat garden has ways of dealing with greenfly, slugs, caterpillars and all the other creatures which the modern gardener calls pests. As soon as the greenfly appear, you will begin to notice little wriggly grey 'maggots' hunting them. They are ladybird larvae, and they can wipe out hundreds and hundreds of greenfly every day. If you spray the greenfly, then you will almost certainly kill their natural predators. Then your roses really will be in trouble, because the 'pests' always recover more quickly than the predators. The other effect of chemicals is even more serious. As I have already explained, all the animals you love best depend on plants or plant-eating animals for food. The hedgehog, for example, will munch its way through dozens of slugs as it snuffles around the garden. The nest-boxful of baby blue tits that you are so proud of, will keep their parents busy collecting hundreds of caterpillars every day. If you are spraying the greenfly, or putting down slug-pellets to kill the slugs, then you will inevitably finish up poisoning the hedgehogs and the baby blue tits as well. In my experience, a garden free from chemicals rarely suffers from any sort of 'epidemic', and certainly I feel much happier about eating fruit and vegetables that I know are free from poisons. One very good way of bringing a boost to the number of 'predators' in your vegetable patch, is to plant some flowers there too. African marigolds, for example, attract large numbers of hoverflies, which then attack the caterpillars that might otherwise eat your cabbages.

Rule 4: Provide lots of breeding sites

If your aim is to have wild creatures living out their lives in your rich-habitat garden, then they will need somewhere safe to breed. The native plants and the decaying leaf litter will keep many of the smaller creatures happy, but you can go quite a bit further. Bring some big lumps of timber into the garden, and build a log-pile. In no time at all this mini-habitat will be alive with all kinds of wood-boring beetles, wood wasps, and grubs of one description or another. In the autumn a host of different toadstools will appear. These are the fruiting parts of the various fungi which are rotting the wood away. If the pile is big enough it will provide hidy-holes for woodmice, spiders will build their webs there, and you may even find a pair of wrens or robins nesting amongst the logs.

Hedgerows are an important part of the breeding habitat for many songbirds and small mammals. Plant a mixture of hawthorn, field maple, wildrose and wild privet, and you'll give yourself a prickly nesting site and a collection of native insect food plants too.

Many British garden birds originally lived in woodland. Given the choice, a lot of them would naturally nest in holes in dead trees or branches, but of course there aren't likely to be many of these sites in your garden. Nesting boxes provide a very good substitute, and it is worth putting up several different types. Some should have small entrance holes – 25mm for blue tits, and a little larger for great tits and starlings – and some should have open fronts, for robins, blackbirds and spotted fly catchers. Make sure they are always out of reach of cats, and never put them in full sun, or the baby birds will get too hot. It is important to clean the boxes out at the end of each breeding season. Otherwise you can get a build up of parasites and the birds will suffer.

Mixing the habitats

The ideal rich-habitat garden will look something like a flowery woodland glade. Plant trees and shrubs, some of them native, along the northern and eastern side of the garden. This will provide some shelter, and create a 'woodland-edge habitat' – very good for songbirds. If you can't manage any trees, then at least plant a hedge, and if that proves difficult, plant climbers such as honeysuckle and ivy to cover the walls and fences.

Once you have a 'woodland' canopy beginning to cast a little dappled shade, begin to introduce some woodland wildflowers. Primroses, violets and foxgloves are easy to grow from seed, and they really are very beautiful. Build up your leaf-litter and dead wood mini-habitats, and put in a couple of nest-boxes for good measure.

Plant up the sunniest part of your glade with masses of flowers and shrubs. This is the main 'service-station' feeding area and it should have something in flower all year round. There is a list of the best garden flowers at the back of the book – but as a rough guide choose large colourful 'single' flowers like petunias, or flowers with lots of pollen or a strong perfume. Don't leave bare earth between the plants. Fill up the garden beds completely, and if you can't afford all the shrubs and perennial plants at first, use lots of hardy annuals. Butterflies love candytuft, and hoverflies will arrive in their hundreds to sunbathe in a good patch of Californian poppies.

Try to build your pond well away from overhanging trees. The fallen leaves will clog it up and turn it smelly and black otherwise. The best spot is a corner which catches the morning sun, but doesn't get baked at mid-day – and do try to have at least one bank with plenty of low cover running back into the shrubbery. This will provide shelter for the more timid creatures that visit your pool. If you have room, extend the pond lining to make a shallow, boggy area too, and then you will be able to grow marsh plants such as meadowsweet, purple loosestrife and marsh-marigold.

The lawn completes the wildlife garden. By all means keep some of it cut short. Close-mown grass is very good for daisies, for picnicking and sunbathing, and it might also help convince your neighbours and friends that the slightly wilder rich-habitat area beyond is supposed to look that way.

Do try letting some of the lawn grow a little longer though, a number of our most beautiful wildflowers grow best in meadows, and we really have lost so many in recent years. Try leaving part of the lawn uncut until July, and then take off a mini hay crop. If you manage that, then you can start to introduce cowslips, selfheal, cat's-ear and all the other spring meadow plants. In fact, you will probably find quite a few of them have been lying there dormant for years. You have simply never allowed them to flower before. If you have room, allow another patch of lawn to grow and flower unmown right through until September. In no time at all you will be able to enjoy late summer wildflowers such as field scabious, knapweed, sorrel and meadow buttercup, and of course you will be providing a marvellous habitat for meadow-brown butterflies, grasshoppers and the like.

Last but not least, don't forget to include a place for *you* – rich-habitat gardens are for sitting in and enjoying. The first rule of nature-watching is to sit very quietly for a few minutes, and let the wildlife accept you. Give yourself one or two sheltered seats, with a good view of the various habitats you have created. Then you can just sit back and watch the garden come to life, comfortable in the knowledge that you're doing something positive and enjoyable to help nature conservation.

Keeping notes

I'm always thrilled when I spot my first butterfly of the year, hear the first cuckoo, see the tadpoles wriggle in their spawn for the first time, and notice that the swifts have left in the autumn, to begin their 5000 mile flight to Africa. The problem is I can never remember if it is earlier or later than the year before. Now there is somewhere to make a note or two.

I hope you will keep this book for a long time. Keep it to hand, and use it to keep a record of your garden wildlife year by year. There is a special page at the back for 'firsts' and a section for weekly records.

Plan For a Wildlife Garden

There is no such thing as a standard garden – thank goodness! Some people may want to turn their whole patch over to meadow, whilst others will want to keep their garden just as it has always been, but perhaps stop using chemical sprays, and allow themselves the luxury of a rotting log-pile habitat out of sight behind the garage. The important thing is to have a go – however timid you may be at first.

This plan is just one suggestion for laying out a small garden to provide a range of habitats for wildlife. There is plenty of diversity; plenty of cover for the more secretive creatures, and plenty of room left for people. If the shrub and flower borders contain a good few native species then there will be a rich community of insects, and the more spectacular creatures will follow. Of course, if you can persuade your neighbours to adopt a similar, more natural approach to gardening, then together you can provide a really valuable contribution to nature-conservation, and have even more birds, butterflies and a whole host of fascinating wildlife to enjoy right outside your back door.

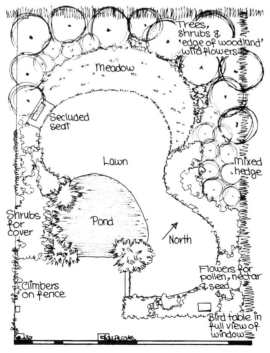

January

It can be very cold in January. This is definitely a month for staying indoors. Out in the wild, most of the natural food supplies will be getting very thin on the ground. Rosehips and hawthorn berries are usually gobbled up before Christmas. This means that your garden can become a real life-saver if you provide a regular supply of food and water for passing wildlife. If you have left plenty of dead leaves under the hedge, and the odd pile of rotting logs dotted around in quiet corners, then in milder moments you'll see plenty of activity, with blackbirds scratching away all day long, wrens and blue tits hopping around picking up tasty morsels, and perhaps even evidence of the odd wandering fox turning over a log here and there, in its search for hidden slugs and beetles.

The really hard weather will often drive unusual visitors into gardens. Some of them, like the foxes, will generally only creep in under cover of darkness, and you will have to look out for telltale tracks in the mud, an unusual pile of droppings or some other evidence to build up an identikit picture of your guests. Muntjac deer, for instance, quite often wander through suburban gardens in January, late at night. You may hear their strange 'bark', and sometimes you catch a glimpse of them in the car headlights, looking for all the world like a fox without a tail. Muntjac love the soft new crimson growth on our prize rose bushes, so if yours have gone missing, look around for the evidence.

The many migratory birds that get blown into our gardens during hard January weather are rather less secretive. Redwings and fieldfares for instance, will often visit the garden, particularly if you throw a few apples onto the lawn. They spend the summer months in Northern Scandinavia and Russia, but as the Arctic winter sets in they migrate south in huge flocks. Most of the time they feed out in the countryside, but when the north east gales blow they move into the shelter of town.

Even on your bird table you are likely to have lots of foreign visitors in winter. We see starlings, blackbirds, robins and several other garden birds all year round, but in fact their numbers are swollen enormously in January and February by flocks of brave birds which migrate from the frozen north to join our residents. There are special winter visitors too, such as redpolls and siskins. Their favourite winter food is alder seed, and siskins have employed the gymnastics they have developed in the wild, to help them feed on bags of peanuts suspended from our garden bird tables. In spring most of these small birds fly to the far north to breed, but it's exciting to think that now, in January, the birds squabbling over the crumbs in your garden may well be Russian or Norwegian.

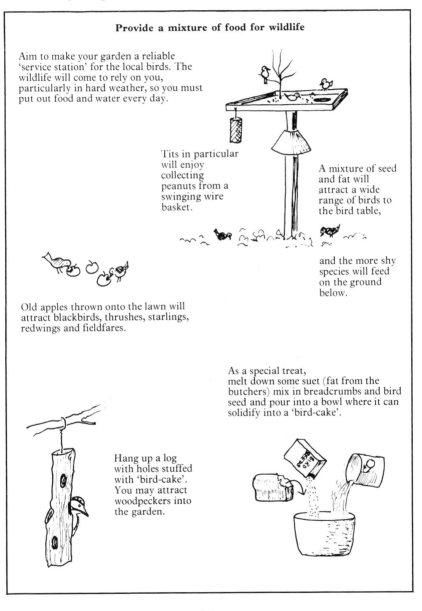

Provide a mixture of food for wildlife

Aim to make your garden a reliable 'service station' for the local birds. The wildlife will come to rely on you, particularly in hard weather, so you must put out food and water every day.

Tits in particular will enjoy collecting peanuts from a swinging wire basket.

A mixture of seed and fat will attract a wide range of birds to the bird table,

and the more shy species will feed on the ground below.

Old apples thrown onto the lawn will attract blackbirds, thrushes, starlings, redwings and fieldfares.

As a special treat, melt down some suet (fat from the butchers) mix in breadcrumbs and bird seed and pour into a bowl where it can solidify into a 'bird-cake'.

Hang up a log with holes stuffed with 'bird-cake'. You may attract woodpeckers into the garden.

February

You may wake up on a cold February morning, to find that snow has fallen overnight. Don't groan. Wrap up warm, pull on your wellies and prepare for a spot of detective work. Even at this time of year, there will be many animals using your garden after dark. Fresh snow will be criss-crossed with tracks, and you might be pleasantly surprised by the clues you find. Foxes, for instance, are really very common in towns, and the straight line of their footprints is an easy one to identify – particularly if it leads to the upturned dustbin.

When the sun does break through in February, it begins to feel as if spring has arrived. You will see the first of your snowdrops and primroses flower this month, and the hazel will be covered in beautiful delicate catkins. There is much more frost and snow still to come of course, but when the birds begin to show an interest in one another, it is a useful reminder to put up some nest-boxes. In the wild, quite a lot of our garden birds would build their nests in holes in trees. Nest-boxes can help make up for the lack of dead trees in towns. Try to avoid nest-boxes which are brightly coloured. The dull brown/green of natural wood is best. You don't want to advertise the nesting birds to predators.

If you have room, put up a range of different nest-boxes. The open-fronted type is popular with robins and blackbirds. The size of hole in the more typical model will determine the kind of bird that nests there. Blue tits will squeeze through a hole as tiny as an inch (25mm) in diameter, and they will chip away for hours if it's too tight for comfort. The bigger the hole, the wider the range of possible users, and the biggest bird that can force its way in usually wins. Enlarge the hole to 2 inches (50mm) and you will mainly find starlings or housesparrows take over.

Keep your nest-boxes out of reach of the local cats. Walls are safer than trees, and never position a box in full sun or the baby birds may overheat. Choose a site within view of a window, and disinfect nest-boxes at the end of each summer.

Make a mini-wetland

A garden pond is a magnet to wildlife. Choose a level, sunny position, in view of the house, away from overhanging trees, and ideally with shrubbery on one edge and open lawn or paving along the rest of the margin.

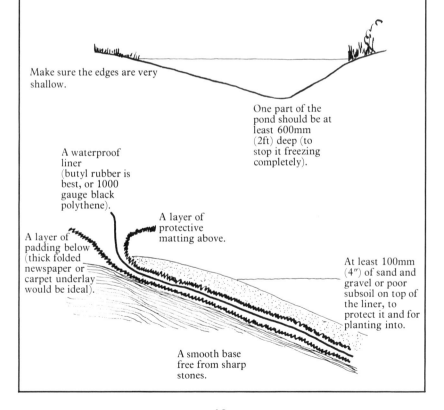

Make sure the edges are very shallow.

One part of the pond should be at least 600mm (2ft) deep (to stop it freezing completely).

A waterproof liner (butyl rubber is best, or 1000 gauge black polythene).

A layer of protective matting above.

A layer of padding below (thick folded newspaper or carpet underlay would be ideal).

At least 100mm (4") of sand and gravel or poor subsoil on top of the liner, to protect it and for planting into.

A smooth base free from sharp stones.

March

The wildlife garden really starts to stir itself in March. The birds are particularly noisy, squabbling over mates and territories, and by the end of the month many of them will have built a nest. When baby birds first hatch, a diet of hard seeds such as peanuts can be harmful. If you have been feeding through the winter, then it is important to restrict the food to fat, and other soft matter, by the end of the month.

If you have a pond in the garden, then the frogs and toads will begin their noisy evening parties in March. The noise they make as the males call for the females to join them is quite surprising the first time you hear it. If you have made a new pond, then you may be lucky enough to have the odd wandering amphibian discover it for himself, but to be sure of success it is well worth introducing some spawn. Try to transfer it from a pond which is either very well supplied, or one which is threatened with destruction. Remember that if you transfer some pond weed at the same time you may inherit a few newt eggs, stuck individually to the leaves, and perhaps one or two long threads of toad spawn, though toads and newts tend to breed a little later than frogs. Don't introduce spawn to ponds with goldfish. Goldfish eat tadpoles.

March is a very good month for planting things. In a small garden, a hedge provides perhaps the best means of introducing native plants, and this is the time to do it. Hawthorn, field maple, yew, native privet, holly, dog rose and beech all make marvellous hedgerow plants. Each of them supports its own particular range of dependent insects (143 in the case of hawthorn for example), and of course, the dense twiggy growth provides good cover for nesting birds, and shy creatures such as the hedgehog and the wood mouse. Plant two-year-old nursery-grown seedlings in blocks, with about 200mm (8 inches) between the plants.

If you have room, plant a tree somewhere. English alder *(Alnus glutinosa)* and silver birch *(Betula pendula)* are both very good for wildlife, and there are native wild cherries, rowan, crab-apple and field maple too – all suitable for gardens.

Even the tiniest garden or terrace has room for a climber or two. Honeysuckle and ivy are the best choices. They both grow quickly, do well in sun or shade, and they provide nectar, edible fruits and valuable cover for wildlife.

You may not think 'weeds' are worth conserving, but in fact some of our most colourful cornfield weeds have almost become extinct since farmers began using chemical sprays. March is the best time to sow seed of these beautiful wildflowers, so take a deep breath, rake over a strip of vegetable patch and sprinkle on a handful of cornfield weed seeds. You'll be thrilled with the colours you get from a mixture of cornflower, poppy, corn marigolds, corncockle and mayweed. They should be a picture by June.

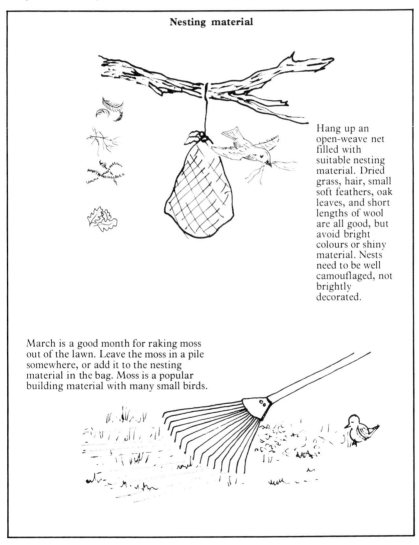

Nesting material

Hang up an open-weave net filled with suitable nesting material. Dried grass, hair, small soft feathers, oak leaves, and short lengths of wool are all good, but avoid bright colours or shiny material. Nests need to be well camouflaged, not brightly decorated.

March is a good month for raking moss out of the lawn. Leave the moss in a pile somewhere, or add it to the nesting material in the bag. Moss is a popular building material with many small birds.

April

April is a month packed full of energy. It's the month when you really feel the world is alive. The nesting season is in full swing, the first butterflies start to appear on sunny days, and this is the time of year when you are likely to see your first swallow, and hear your first cuckoo.

One thing you really must do in April is crawl outside into the garden, at least once, in time to hear the dawn chorus. In early April the battle over nesting territories reaches fever pitch amongst garden song-birds. You need to be up at least an hour before dawn to catch the first song, but the magic of that moment is unforgettable. The thrill you will feel as the traffic-free early morning silence is gradually replaced by the almost deafening music of wrens, blackbirds, thrushes, dunnocks, robins, and so on, will make you tingle with excitement. By 5.30 it is all over. The traffic noise begins its own dawn chorus, and you can creep sleepily back to bed.

Birds aren't the only creatures breeding in April of course. Bats will move from their cold, north-facing hibernation roosts about this time, to set up breeding colonies behind the tile hanging or the weatherboarding of sunny south-facing buildings. You'll do these fascinating creatures a great service by putting up a bat box on a sunny wall, and they will return the favour by gobbling up thousands of midges and other small insects on the balmy summer evenings when you want to sit outside until late.

If you have a new pond in the garden, then April is the best month for introducing waterplants. Marginal species such as flag iris and flowering rush have some new growth to 'get hold of' and as the water warms up, oxygenators get off to a vigorous start.

April is the month for light showers and sunny interludes. This combination brings out a great many of our more secretive creatures. Nip into the garden between showers and see how many different types of slugs and snails you can count. Their colouring is wonderful, and you should be relieved to see that most of them *are not* eating your vegetables.

Spring flowers are important, not simply because primroses, bluebells and forget-me-nots are beautiful wildlife in themselves, but also because their pollen and nectar are vital for the newly emerging insects. Look out for the odd small tortoiseshell sipping nectar from the wallflowers. It needs that sugary boost after its winter hibernation, to give it the energy to find a mate, and then lay its eggs on the young shoots in the nettle patch. Butterflies seem to prefer mauve and purple flowers, and one of the best at this time of year is honesty. Sow a few seeds now, and you'll have flowers for next spring, and lots of attractive seedheads for the bullfinches the following autumn.

The more delicate of our summer garden flowers should be planted in April too. Some are much better for wildlife than others, so choose carefully. As a general rule, double flowers produce very little pollen. Many of them are sterile and provide no seed at all. Go for single varieties of such colourful plants as petunias and dahlia, or heavily perfumed species such as tobacco plant (Nicotiana) and the pretty little white alyssum. Bumblebees are fun to watch, as they use their weight to open the jaws of snapdragons. Sunflowers are a must because they provide lots of nectar and pollen for bees and butterflies, and then go on to provide a rich harvest of seeds which attracts the tits and the finches in early autumn. Make a note of the summer flowers which attract most insects in other people's gardens, and then plant those the following year.

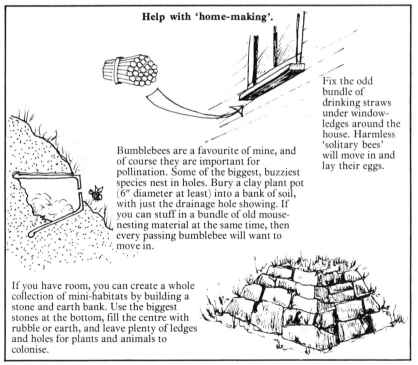

Help with 'home-making'.

Fix the odd bundle of drinking straws under window-ledges around the house. Harmless 'solitary bees' will move in and lay their eggs.

Bumblebees are a favourite of mine, and of course they are important for pollination. Some of the biggest, buzziest species nest in holes. Bury a clay plant pot (6″ diameter at least) into a bank of soil, with just the drainage hole showing. If you can stuff in a bundle of old mouse-nesting material at the same time, then every passing bumblebee will want to move in.

If you have room, you can create a whole collection of mini-habitats by building a stone and earth bank. Use the biggest stones at the bottom, fill the centre with rubble or earth, and leave plenty of ledges and holes for plants and animals to colonise.

May

In early May you are likely to see a whole host of summer-visiting birds for the first time. By keeping a record from year to year, you can see how regular the pattern is. It is amazing to know that the swallows, swifts and housemartins swooping over your garden have flown ten thousand miles – to Southern Africa and back – and have managed to return to the very spot where they were hatched. If you can persuade just one pair of these wonderful birds to nest in or around your house, you will have made an important international contribution to nature conservation. There are special nest-box designs for swifts and housemartins, but swallows simply need a safe shelf or ledge in a building with the door or window left open. There will be other summer visitors in and around your garden now, too. Listen for the call of the cuckoo. It's just possible that the dunnock nesting in your garden hedge may provide one of this season's foster homes. Summer visitors such as the willow and garden warblers produce some of the most musical of garden songs. One of the latest arrivals, the spotted flycatcher, will often nest close to a door or window if you provide a safe little platform, well camouflaged by climbing plants. This delightful little bird will spend day after day sitting on the same twig or fence post, and occasionally fluttering up into the air, snapping up a fly and then returning to its perch.

The pond will be changing dramatically throughout this month. The endless supply of moisture makes waterside plants grow very quickly, and the water itself will be teeming with life. The most obvious residents will be the tadpoles, often being chased by waterboatman and diving beetle larvae. Little black whirlygig beetles seem to appear from nowhere, and whizz round and round like miniature dodgem cars. Pond skaters are fascinating to watch, galloping over the surface of the water to investigate anything that feels like a struggling prospective meal. May is also the month when the first of the dragonflies appear. Some of our bigger species are enormous – 150mm (6″) in length, and they come in a dazzling variety of colours – blue, green, red and brown.

The songthrush is normally a rather shy bird, although it probably wins the competition for best songster in the dawn chorus. At this time of year though, it may suddenly become more noticeable. Songthrushes love to eat snails. Once they have young nestlings to feed they are far too busy to indulge themselves, but in the calm period before the eggs hatch, you will often see your thrushes hunting out garden snails, bringing them one by one to a particular 'anvil' – usually a lump of stone or a paving slab – and bashing them over and over again until the shell cracks, and then the bird can gobble up the juicy contents.

Most wild creatures have fascinating feeding habits if you care to watch closely. Many plants rely on animals to spread their seed. There are well known examples of course – squirrels and jays absentmindedly burying acorns, blackbirds helping hawthorn seeds to germinate by digesting the soft fleshy fruit around them. In May, if you look very closely, you can see one of the most remarkable of these partnerships. Primrose seed, which ripens this month, has a waxy coating which ants seem to find irresitible. If your primroses have flowered well, watch the seed heads for a minute or two and you will probably see an ant nip in, pick up a seed and carry it off. Once the coating has been stripped off, the seed is left to germinate and produce a new seedling.

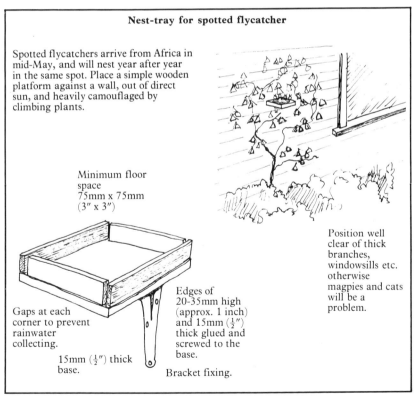

Nest-tray for spotted flycatcher

Spotted flycatchers arrive from Africa in mid-May, and will nest year after year in the same spot. Place a simple wooden platform against a wall, out of direct sun, and heavily camouflaged by climbing plants.

Minimum floor space 75mm x 75mm (3" x 3")

Position well clear of thick branches, windowsills etc. otherwise magpies and cats will be a problem.

Gaps at each corner to prevent rainwater collecting.

15mm ($\frac{1}{2}$") thick base.

Edges of 20-35mm high (approx. 1 inch) and 15mm ($\frac{1}{2}$") thick glued and screwed to the base.

Bracket fixing.

June

June is the month when many plants stop growing so vigorously and start to flower like mad. Along with this blaze of flower-colour comes a real boom in the number of garden insects. In a 'good year' when the spring has been reasonably dry, butterflies and bumblebees will bring the sunny June garden to life. Adult butterflies will feed on nectar from a wide range of flowers and it is worth keeping a record of the ones they seem to prefer. They are much more choosy about where to lay their eggs, however. Almost all species of butterflies and moths have caterpillars which can eat the leaves of only one or two species of plant. Unless we conserve these larval food plants then our butterflies will disappear. Wildlife gardeners can do a great deal to help with this aspect of conservation. The common blue butterfly must lay its eggs on the leaves of birdsfoot trefoil, clover or black medick; the orange tip's caterpillars can feed only on honesty, sweetrocket, milkmaids or hedge mustard; the meadow brown butterfly must have uncut leaves of meadow grasses, and of course the spectacular small tortoiseshell and peacock butterflies, much as they may love sipping the nectar from buddleias and michaelmas daisies, can only survive from generation to generation if we make sure their caterpillars have stinging nettles to feed on. In fact there are two generations of small tortoiseshells each year, and you can do your resident population a great service by cutting down some of the local nettles early this month. New, soft green shoots will quickly spring up and this is where the second brood of butterfly eggs will be laid.

With so many creatures buzzing around in the garden, it is very tempting to start spraying everything in sight. Aim instead to achieve a natural balance in your garden. If you provide plenty of cover, a fair amount of dead wood, some of the more attractive native plants and access to water, then you will build up the populations of predatory animals. These are the creatures that kill the pest species.

Every garden has greenfly in it in June. If you resist the temptation to spray, then you will begin to notice that ladybirds and their wriggly grey larvae increase and so do the beautiful green lacewings. Each one of these predators will munch its way through hundreds of greenfly every day. If you spray to kill the pests then you are very likely to kill their natural enemies, too. Within a week or two the pest will have bounced back to epidemic proportions and will be free to chew up your garden undisturbed. All of our most popular garden wildlife species depend ultimately on plants, and the unpopular creepy crawlies that eat them. The blue tits we lovingly care for throughout the winter, must feed caterpillars and greenfly to their newly-hatched babies. Spray the pest and you poison the birds. June is the month when hedgehogs are most in evidence, shuffling noisily around the garden. If your listen carefully you'll hear an occasional juicy crunch in the undergrowth — another slug meeting with a sticky end. Poison the slugs and you poison the hedgehogs.

If April is the month for early morning meditation, then June is certainly the month for enjoying the garden at night. Choose a balmy, slightly overcast evening, find a comfortable spot with a good view of the garden, and the breeze blowing into your face, and just sit quietly. As darkness falls you will hear the garden begin to wake up. Bats will be out at dusk. Moths will begin to emerge from the long grass and feed around the honeysuckle and the evening primroses, and you will hear mice squeaking, hedgehogs crashing and shuffling around, and perhaps an owl calling, just to complete the scene.

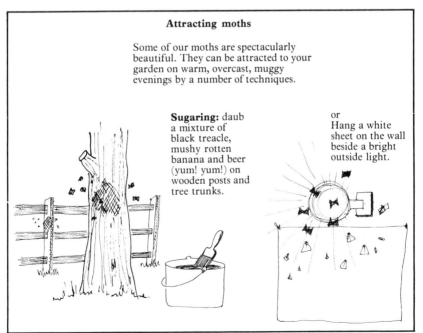

Attracting moths

Some of our moths are spectacularly beautiful. They can be attracted to your garden on warm, overcast, muggy evenings by a number of techniques.

Sugaring: daub a mixture of black treacle, mushy rotten banana and beer (yum! yum!) on wooden posts and tree trunks.

or
Hang a white sheet on the wall beside a bright outside light.

July

This is the month when the soft fruit ripens. Blackbirds, squirrels and several other creatures enjoy raspberries and blackcurrants every bit as much as we do, so if you want any for yourself, put a net over the fruit without delay.

Many of the yellow flowers bloom in July. It's a sunny month. Buttercups look a picture in the countryside, and in the flower garden the first of the marigolds and sunflowers will be blazing away. Look carefully, and you will soon notice that the marigolds in particular are very popular with lots of little insects which look like wasps. Most of them are hoverflies. They are quite harmless, but fascinating to study. Many of the different common species lay their eggs in the caterpillars and grubs of garden pest species, and when their own eggs hatch, the hoverfly larvae kill and eat the pest. For this reason it is well worth growing a few rows of marigolds amongst your vegetables. They will help attract more predators, control the pests and so allow you to enjoy non-sprayed vegetables.

The better known stinging wasp which hoverflies are mimicking is also an extremely useful insect in the garden. The adults are important pollinators of course, but they also kill enormous numbers of garden pests each summer. Keep your eyes open and you will see adult wasps catch flies and various grubs, and fly back to their nests to feed their catch to the wasp-larvae.

Yet another group of wasps is responsible for many of the neat little holes which appear in your fence posts, and in the rotting-log habitat you have provided in your wildlife garden. These wood-boring wasps come in several shapes and sizes, and they will provide hours of fascinating entertainment when you are looking for an excuse to sit quietly and enjoy the sun.

July is the month when the adult newts will leave your pond. They wander off, generally at night when the grass is wet with dew, and may roam for a mile or two, but they will almost always return to the same pond to breed the following spring, after spending the cold winter months in hibernation under a rotting log or in a crack in a wall somewhere. The baby newts, the froglets and tiny new toads should mostly be fully formed by now, but they generally stay in the pond for at least a further month. When they do leave they may stay away for two or three years, but once they are old enough to breed they too will find their way back to their original pond.

This is the month when most of the dragonflies lay their eggs. If

28

your pond is large you may have several different species breeding there. Watch them carefully. They all have quite different techniques for mating and choose different parts of the pond to lay their eggs.

If you've been brave enough to let part of the lawn grow wild, then July is the month when you should 'harvest' the hay. You must cut the meadow at least once annually and if the wildflowers are to get better each year then you must rake off the clippings. If you are too lazy to bother, then the fertility will build up, the coarse grasses will thrive, and your flowery meadow will quickly turn into a weedy jungle.

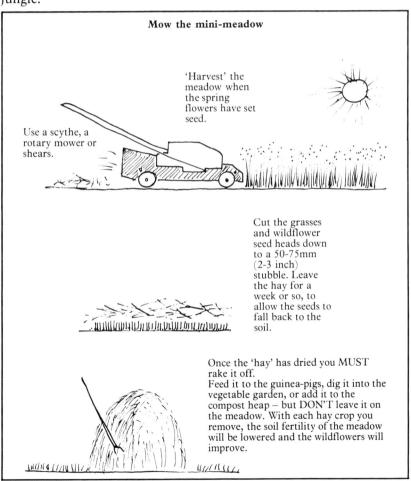

Mow the mini-meadow

'Harvest' the meadow when the spring flowers have set seed.

Use a scythe, a rotary mower or shears.

Cut the grasses and wildflower seed heads down to a 50-75mm (2-3 inch) stubble. Leave the hay for a week or so, to allow the seeds to fall back to the soil.

Once the 'hay' has dried you MUST rake it off.
Feed it to the guinea-pigs, dig it into the vegetable garden, or add it to the compost heap – but DON'T leave it on the meadow. With each hay crop you remove, the soil fertility of the meadow will be lowered and the wildflowers will improve.

August

August can be very hot and very dry. If it is, then your pond will be the centre of attention for wildlife, both by day and by night. If you haven't a pond, then do at least try and set up a bird bath. A dustbin lid placed upside down on a few bricks is very good – just the right kind of gently shelving shoreline. You'll quickly be rewarded by happy holiday crowds of bathing birds.

A well-balanced garden pond will also be popular with wildlife for another reason. Clouds of small flying insects are likely to emerge in August. You might think that would be a menace – midge bites galore. In fact in a wildlife garden they simply add to the entertainment by drawing in highly efficient predators. By day the dragonflies will patrol close to the water surface, and snap up a good many midges. Once word gets round there will be swallows racing backwards and forwards over the pond, swooping down occasionally to snatch a drink, and eating several thousand insects in the course of a day. As night falls you may well have pipistrelle bats moving in, silently whizzing round and round about three feet above the surface, mopping up any unlucky stragglers.

On really hot days most of the larger creatures will find a shady spot and just try to keep cool. You will see blackbirds, for instance, seizing the opportunity for a spot of personal hygiene. The heat down amongst the feathers must presumably become unbearable for their parasites, and you can watch as they peck and scratch to clean themselves. Many birds will also take a dust bath in hot weather, all too often choosing a neatly-raked seed bed in the vegetable patch to do it. If you're really lucky you may see a mistlethrush or a blackbird 'anting'. The bird squats on the ground, with wings outstretched, and encourages ants to crawl all over it. These little insects produce a strong (formic) acid, and this probably helps rid the bird of irritating mites.

Ants do something else which is fascinating in August. On the first hot day, usually around the middle of the afternoon, the whole neighbourhood suddenly becomes alive with flying ants. If you are lucky enough to be in the garden when it happens, watch carefully. At precisely the same time over hundreds of square miles, and certainly in several spots in your garden, all the little male ants and the relatively huge fertile queens will emerge from their nests under the lawn and the paving slabs. Both sexes have wings. They fly up in clouds, mate in mid-air and then the fertilised females land again.

30

They immediately bite off their wings, and then crawl into a sheltered spot and start a new colony. The whole spectacle takes less than fifteen minutes, and only happens once each year, so you can easily miss it, but once you've seen the amazing, magical performance, with its perfectly co-ordinated cast of millions, you'll never want to kill ants ever again. Needless to say, with so many redundant males staggering around after the party, it won't be long before the garden is equally alive with birds pecking away in all directions and hardly able to believe their luck.

Collecting wildflower seeds

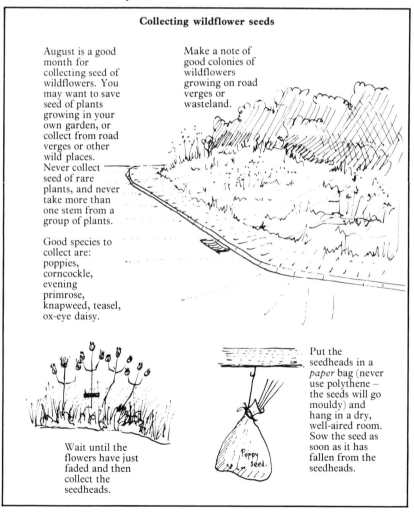

August is a good month for collecting seed of wildflowers. You may want to save seed of plants growing in your own garden, or collect from road verges or other wild places. Never collect seed of rare plants, and never take more than one stem from a group of plants.

Good species to collect are: poppies, corncockle, evening primrose, knapweed, teasel, ox-eye daisy.

Make a note of good colonies of wildflowers growing on road verges or wasteland.

Wait until the flowers have just faded and then collect the seedheads.

Put the seedheads in a *paper* bag (never use polythene – the seeds will go mouldy) and hang in a dry, well-aired room. Sow the seed as soon as it has fallen from the seedheads.

31

September

This is the month when our summer visitors leave us to spend a warmer winter further south. Swifts will team up in squadrons to scream round and round the rooftops, and then suddenly they are gone, the young ones leaving a week or two before their parents, and miraculously finding their own way to southern Africa by instinct. Swallows gather on the telegraph wires – parents and young all together, stocked up with millions of insects and ready for the long flight. Housemartins have a slightly more staggered departure. You may well notice young birds fluttering up under the eaves, presumably looking for possible nest sites, and this is perhaps the moment when an artificial housemartin nest-box is earmarked as a breeding site for the following spring.

There are still plenty of butterflies around in September. If you deadhead the buddleia you can usually encourage it to keep on producing new flowers into early autumn, and those butterflies which overwinter as hibernating adults will be glad of the strength-giving nectar. The small tortoiseshell and the peacock are both fond of hibernating indoors, but the brimstone, that beautiful yellow insect from which all butterflies are thought to take their name, is perfectly camouflaged to look like an old dead ivy leaf. At the first touch of frost the brimstones hang themselves up amongst the sheltering leaves of any ivy-covered tree or building, and 'disappear' until the warmer weather returns. Amongst the border plants, michaelmas daisies and the ice plant, *Sedum spectabile*, are both extremely good for butterflies, and on a warm September day you may find dozens of insects stocking up with nectar and showing off their brightly coloured wings in the sun. The cooler weather at this time of year makes them much dopier, and easier to creep close to.

Most gardeners chop down the seedheads in the flower garden about now. In a wildlife garden the seedheads are as important as the flowers. Leave them standing as long as you can, and stake them against the late summer gales if necessary. Golden rod will be seeding by now, and you should also have seedheads on the sunflowers.

Generally speaking the birds will leave the seedheads alone while food is plentiful, but at the first sign of frost, the goldfinches and bullfinches in particular, will move in and start feeding. This is when the teasel really comes into its own. It is a tall elegant biennial, and is worth growing from seed each year just for its purple flowers, but

Spring Wildflowers

Above left: Greater celandine with red campion in the background. Both will happily seed in a woodland habitat. Ants strip off the waxy coating of greater celandine seeds and help the plant to spread.

Above right: Sow foxglove seeds one year to flower the next and sow 2 years in a row to establish a colony. Bumble bees love them.

Right: Apple blossom, lilac, tulips, wallflowers and forget-me-nots all help boost the 'service station' food supply for newly-emerged insects.

Below left: Primroses and speedwell. A lovely combination of colours and an important source of early nectar and pollen for insects.

Below right: Several butterflies lay their eggs on the leaves of violets. Oxlips only occur naturally in a few places now; your garden can help in their conservation.

Early Summer Wildflowers

Top left: Field scabious. A pretty meadow flower for the garden. Very popular with butterflies and bees.

Top middle: Corn cockle. Beautiful native cornfield weed now almost extinct in the wild. Grows very easily from seed.

Top right: Thyme needs a well drained gritty soil and positively hums with bumble bees.

Right: The wildlife garden should ideally comprise a woodland glade with a sunny meadow and pool surrounded by cool shady shrubberies and flower borders.

Bottom left: Yellow flag iris and ragged robin. Damsel flies are attracted to the irises.

Bottom right: Hawkweed is one of the wildflowers which often springs up when you start meadow gardening.

Autumn Wildflowers

Above: The first frosts of autumn are a reminder of the hard times ahead. Planting the right shrubs and flowers provides a rich supply of seeds and fruits for birds and other creatures to enjoy.

Below left: You must grow teasels in your wildlife garden. The pollen from their tall elegant flowers turns the bumble bees pink and in the autumn charms of gold finches will feed on the seeds.

Below, top right: The fruit of lords and ladies or cuckoo pint which provides a bright splash of colour in the autumn and will happily colonise at the bottom of your hedge.

Below, bottom right: Try growing wild strawberries. The fruits are tiny but deliciously sweet so you will have to be quick to get there before the blackbirds, squirrels and wood mice.

Garden Flowers

Above and opposite page below: The 'service station' of my wildlife garden is full of cottage garden plants which are colourful and rich in nectar and pollen; many of them produce a heavy crop of seed as well.

Below, top left: Shrub roses provide a heavy crop of rose hips for the birds to feed on in autumn.

Below, bottom left: Many of the culinary herbs are very good for garden wildlife. Borage has beautiful flowers which bumble bees and honey bees find irresistible. Try letting some of your parsley and mint flower too.

Below, top right: Buddleia, otherwise known as the 'butterfly plant'.

Below, bottom right: Try to provide plenty of flowers in the autumn. The small tortoiseshell, that hibernates in the winter, will benefit from a last minute supply of nectar from Michaelmas daisies.

Above left: Damsel flies often climb up the leaves of flag irises before bursting out of their underwater skins. Look around the base of the stems for empty damsel fly husks.

Above, top right: Choose garden flowers that are rich in pollen and nectar. Shasta daisies are popular with hoverflies. The taller evening primroses open their flowers as the sun goes down and attract clouds of night-flying moths.

Above, bottom right: Tobacco plants are available for summer bedding from every garden centre. They look beautiful, have a marvellous evening perfume and attract a wide range of night-flying insects.

Meadow Habitat

Above: My patch of meadow was created by sowing a mixture of fine grasses and meadow flower seed.

Below, top left: Create a habitat that's rich in plant-eating creepy crawlies and you'll quickly attract predators such as kestrels.

Below, bottom left: Speedwell and lady's smock are two early spring meadow flowers. Lady's smock is particularly valuable in the wildlife garden as its flowers attract many butterflies and the orange tip lays its eggs on the leaves.

Below, top right: Snakes-head fritillaries are almost extinct in the wild but you can now buy corms from garden centres.

Below, bottom right: Cowslips were once familiar wild flowers; try growing them in your garden.

Woodland Edge Habitat

Top left: Hedgehogs can be encouraged to visit with a saucer of milk or a constant supply of slugs, earthworms and snails.

Top right: Many of our garden song birds were originally forest species. Great tits would naturally nest in holes in trees but will readily nest in a box.

Right: My small group of old logs provides a home for an amazing range of wild life. Toadstools appear every autumn and wild flowers thrive in this habitat too.

Below left: It is very important to give yourself a quiet spot to sit in. That is the best way to enjoy your garden wildlife.

Below right: On the edge of woodland, a mixture of red campion, bluebells and leopards-bane provides a splash of colour in early spring.

Water Habitat

Above left: Garden ponds have helped to save frogs from disappearing.

Above right: Red hot poker makes a suitable perch for a broad-bodied darter dragonfly which must have a pond to lay its eggs in.

Right: In the heat of summer the pond has a lovely cooling effect on the whole garden.

Below left: A large-white butterfly feeding from the flowers of purple loosestrife.

Below middle: Ragged robin grows in damp meadows and marshes. Land drainage has made this a very rare plant in the wild.

Below right: My artificial marsh is only about 6 ft. square but provides an ideal habitat for meadowsweet, marsh marigold and purple loosestrife.

when the bumblebees have done their job, and the seed has ripened, the spiky seedhead becomes an irresistible magnet for goldfinches. These are perhaps our most brilliantly colourful garden birds; they are relatively common in towns, move around in flocks known as charms, and they just love teasels.

Many other wild fruits are at their best in September too. Bramble is a marvellous plant for wildlife all year round, providing prickly shelter, a blossom rich in pollen, and leaves which feed a whole host of native insects. The blackberries though, are the bramble's crowning glory. They bring a real splash of autumn colour to the hedgerow, and they are a favourite food for blackbirds, thrushes and woodmice. The elderberry fruits in September too, and its popularity, particularly with starlings, is obvious when you see the purple staining on the pavement beneath their roosts.

The end of September is a good time to give the meadow a final tidy up for the winter. In a wet summer there will be quite a lot of regrowth after the June 'harvest', and this needs cutting and raking off. Try to mow this September crop to keep at least 3″ of stubble, and leave the clippings for a few days before removing them. This will allow the grassland insects to migrate down amongst the roots and out of harm's way. This is also the time of year for planting spring bulbs, and if you plant lots of winter aconites, snowdrops and crocuses, they will provide a springtime splash of colour for ever after, and a valuable boost of precious pollen for those hibernating insects which stumble out on the odd sunny days we sometimes get in January and February.

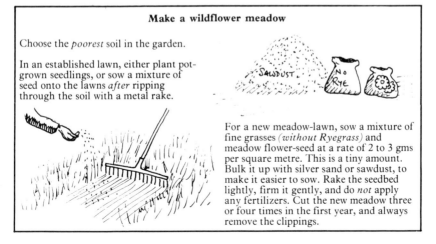

Make a wildflower meadow

Choose the *poorest* soil in the garden.

In an established lawn, either plant pot-grown seedlings, or sow a mixture of seed onto the lawns *after* ripping through the soil with a metal rake.

For a new meadow-lawn, sow a mixture of fine grasses *(without Ryegrass)* and meadow flower-seed at a rate of 2 to 3 gms per square metre. This is a tiny amount. Bulk it up with silver sand or sawdust, to make it easier to sow. Rake the seedbed lightly, firm it gently, and do *not* apply any fertilizers. Cut the new meadow three or four times in the first year, and always remove the clippings.

October

Everything changes in October. It begins to get very cold at night, the autumn colours come to the leaves, and your garden wildlife begins to rely more and more on your kindness to boost its food supply. Every wildlife garden should have a bird-table, and now is the time to start using it.

If you have a pond, it will quickly become black and smelly if it is allowed to fill up with rotting leaves. It may be a bit of a fiddle, but it is well worth covering the pond with netting whilst the autumn leaves are blowing around. Stretch the net tightly over the water, weight it down with bricks, and as the leaves build up, bundle them together and cart them away from the pool. Fallen leaves can be extremely useful in other parts of the wildlife garden. Many creatures feed on dead leaves, and if you pile them up in a sheltered corner then you may well find that hedgehogs and other small mammals will snuggle down amongst them and hibernate for the winter. If you don't have a quiet corner to leave them in over winter, then simply spread them over the surface of the flower borders. Earthworms will gradually drag them down into the soil, but in the meantime, they will help keep down the weeds. The blackbirds, robins and dunnocks will spend all winter scratching around amongst them, looking for mini-beasts to feed on.

By mid-October, most flowers have finished but one particularly important wildlife plant is only just beginning. The common ivy is a marvellous plant in many ways, but its flowers are particularly important as a rich source of autumn nectar. The sweet sticky droplets glisten in the October sun, and on bright days a mature ivy plant will be alive with the buzz of hoverflies, and decorated with the brilliant colour of lingering small tortoiseshells and other over-wintering butterflies. In fact, one species of butterfly, the holly blue, depends on the flowers and young shoots of ivy to feed its autumn brood of caterpillars. The chrysalises then hang dormant amongst the ivy leaves through the winter. When the pretty little butterflies emerge in the spring, they mate and lay their spring brood of eggs on the flower buds of holly.

If there are cold north-east winds in October, then you may well see your first winter visitors this month. Certainly the pond in the park will have newly-arrived migratory ducks and geese from the frozen north. Many of the starlings and tits that you thought were your summer regulars may well, in fact, be winter visitors. The easiest migrants to recognise, though, are those large thrush-like birds, the redwing and the fieldfare. In mild autumns they stay further north until the first snows, but quite often a sudden gale will drive them south into our parks and gardens, where they feast on fallen apples or strip the berries from hawthorn and holly. The redwing is a mild-mannered, shy bird, but the handsome grey and speckled fieldfare is a real bully. If it is a good year for apples, try storing some when they are cheap. As the weather gets harder they will prove a great success in bringing wild birds into the garden.

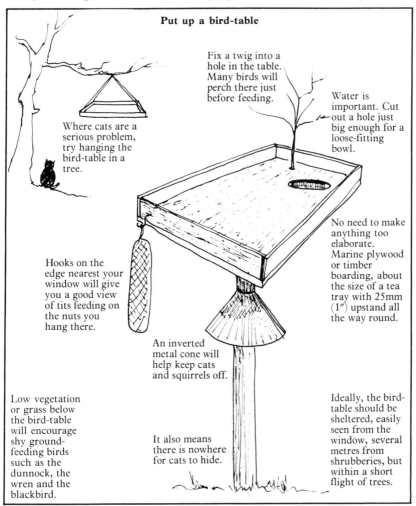

Put up a bird-table

Fix a twig into a hole in the table. Many birds will perch there just before feeding.

Water is important. Cut out a hole just big enough for a loose-fitting bowl.

Where cats are a serious problem, try hanging the bird-table in a tree.

No need to make anything too elaborate. Marine plywood or timber boarding, about the size of a tea tray with 25mm (1″) upstand all the way round.

Hooks on the edge nearest your window will give you a good view of tits feeding on the nuts you hang there.

An inverted metal cone will help keep cats and squirrels off.

Low vegetation or grass below the bird-table will encourage shy ground-feeding birds such as the dunnock, the wren and the blackbird.

It also means there is nowhere for cats to hide.

Ideally, the bird-table should be sheltered, easily seen from the window, several metres from shrubberies, but within a short flight of trees.

November

Traditionally, this is the month for tidying up the garden. Bonfires are generally the order of the day, and gardening experts will tell you to clear away all dead stems and leaf-litter, to prevent the spread of disease.

All that has got to change. Wildlife gardening gives you the perfect excuse for being a little less tidy. Dead wood, seedheads, leaf-mould and decay are all very important indeed to the balanced ecology of the garden. In fact, perhaps the most valuable contribution any gardener can make to nature conservation is to leave room for a little decay.

Ideally, you should have a secluded corner, out of the gaze of neighbours, where things can be allowed to get a bit messy. Make a point of stacking unwanted logs and other timber here, and you will quickly and dramatically boost the wildlife population in your garden. At this time of year a whole display of colourful toadstools will appear too, and if the pile is big enough it will shelter hedgehogs, woodmice, wrens and possibly even a fox or two. This particular kind of habitat gets better and better the longer it remains undisturbed. If you have had one at the back of your shed for years, and were always rather ashamed of it, now you know that it has been serving your local wildlife, even if it has been an embarrassment to everyone else.

November is a good time to start a compost heap. We produce such a lot of kitchen waste in a year, and if you build a proper open-sided compost bin and put a few of those rotting branches in the bottom of it now, the cabbage stems, eggshells and grass clippings will all be turned into useful compost by next autumn. Compost heaps are a marvellous wildlife facility too. They provide a treasure-house of little red worms, grubs and a whole host of other decay organisms. These in turn, attract the attention of hedgehogs, shrews and garden birds.

A good compost heap gets very warm too as the greenery decomposes, and this makes it a favourite breeding site for slow-worms and grass snakes. Environmentally compost heaps are a much better way of disposing of garden weeds too. Bonfires are such a waste.

As you do inevitably tidy up a little for the winter, give some thought to the creation of nesting sites. Nest-boxes can be put in position at this time of year and may well provide a welcome roosting site for small birds, mammals, moths and butterflies on cold winter nights. With a bit of imagination you can provide a whole collection of "casual suggestions" for nesting birds as you put tools away and stack materials. Wrens and robins both nest in containers. The kettle in the hedge bottom really does work surprisingly often. There are lots of other containers you can position in sheltered corners. Put a few wisps of dead grass into your nest sites. This often seems to help the birds cotton on to the idea. Blackbirds and robins will often nest in garden sheds if the window or door is permanently ajar, and favourite nesting sites seem to be the tops of rolls of wire netting, or loops of rope hanging on the wall. Use your imagination. You may well get a pleasant surprise next spring.

Decay and dead wood habitat.

Don't burn the old dead wood, leaf-sweepings and herbaceous border rubbish. Add soft stems to the compost heap, pile old logs in a quiet corner, where they can become overgrown and rot down gradually.

Push leaf-sweepings under the hedge or into the shrubbery – they provide a valuable habitat for invertebrates, birds will scratch amongst them through the winter, and small mammals like the hedgehog will hibernate there.

December

The very short days and the long cold nights of December make life pretty uncomfortable. The ground quite often stays frozen for days on end, and so food and water become critical to survival. Make sure there is always fresh water available, at ground level as well as on the bird-table. Provide a wide range of food for the birds. If you have a park or woodland anywhere near by, then it is worth hanging up a suet log at this time of year, as a temptation to passing woodpeckers. A silver birch log is best, and if you drill a few big holes in it and stuff them with a mixture of fat and seeds, you're really quite likely to be visited by a greater spotted woodpecker on cold December days. Beware though. They have been known to practise their 'drilling' on gateposts, and even to chop through the leg of a bird table on occasion.

Keep some part of your pond-surface unfrozen at all times. Certainly the birds will be grateful, and for some reason there seems to be maximum enthusiasm for bathing, particularly amongst the starlings, on the iciest of days. You need to keep a gap in the ice too, to prevent gases from building up and poisoning the pond life.

December is a good month for pruning trees and shrubs. One way of maintaining a plentiful supply of the leaves of native shrubs and trees in a small garden is to grow several of them as coppiced shrubs. You may not have room for full-grown specimens of such things as field maple, bird cherry, wild gean, hornbeam, white willow, beech and oak. Lack of space may prevent you from enjoying their flowers and fruit, but most of their dependent insects and other resident creatures simply need a plentiful supply of tender leaves. If you cut any of these trees or shrubs down to the ground in December, then they will spring up again the following spring and provide you with a crop of vigorous shoots, and ample food for an enormous range of caterpillars and other leaf-eaters.

December is a very good month to give some thought to nature conservation beyond the garden. The wildlife you enjoy on your doorstep will be as rich or as poor as the environment of your neighbourhood. If your local park has an acre or two of meadow wildflowers in it, then you will have far more chance of attracting brown and skipper butterflies to your own mini-meadow. If there are dead branches on the trees in the churchyard, then bats and woodpeckers will be much more frequent visitors to your patch. Your garden wildlife depends as much on the nettles and brambles of the railway embankment and the marshy settlement tanks of the sewage farm as it does on your peanuts and michaelmas daisies. Spend some of the long December evenings looking at the local large-scale ordnance survey map, and see if you can pick out the neighbourhood's wildlife corridors. Write to your local councillors, the parks director and perhaps the headteacher at the local school, to make sure that they know how important the local green spaces are to you and your wildlife. One of the simplest and most useful things you can do is support your local Nature Conservation Trust. Every county has one, and they will work on your behalf to keep your area green, and to secure a safe place for nature.

Keep the pond ice-free

Try to keep an area of water unfrozen during cold weather.

In really icy weather, pour hot water onto the ice, or renew the water on the bird-table frequently.

Float a dark-coloured soft rubber ball on the pond, or a chunk or two of wood.

Keep the area at the edge of the pond open for bird-bathing and for small mammals to drink from.

All being well, by December you will have a fascinating record of a year of wildlife in your garden. A single year is interesting enough in itself, but your wildlife gardening notes will become more and more enjoyable to read as you begin to build up a picture of the wildlife pattern year by year. You will begin to look forward impatiently to the return of *your* swallows each year. You will be able to provide food for more and more butterflies as you learn about the plants they prefer. You will get a real thrill when the first adult dragonflies emerge from your pond as much as four summers after you saw them laid as eggs on the damp mud at the edge.

Wildlife gardening is very important. It is your chance to do something really useful for nature conservation, and to enjoy yourself into the bargain, and the most exciting thing of all is that a whole new year of repeat performances and first experiences begins again in January.

Oh! and if you are wondering about the ideal Christmas present to buy for your garden wildlife – how about a large, noisy bell for the cat next door!

How To fill in Your Notebook

I hope you will keep this book somewhere handy, so that you can jot down the wildlife events in your own garden 'as they happen'. I use my notebook for two kinds of 'events'. Firstly, it is nice to build up a picture of the date certain things happen year after year. I keep a note of when the first snowdrop opens, when the blue tits first start showing an interest in the nest boxes, the date when the housemartins reappear, and a whole range of other 'milestones' that make up the natural year.

The second kind of note I keep is just a simple record of interesting things I see from day to day. Keeping all those observations in one place makes it easier to jog my memory. Over the years there have been spectacular things, like the June day when a Muntjac deer appeared from nowhere, and idly munched at my bluebells, the evening when magnificent specimens of elephant Hawkmoth *and* a lime Hawkmoth appeared at the kitchen window together, and the unbelievably noisy half hour two hedgehogs spent mating in the flowerbed. There are interesting details that I want to keep a note of too. I've watched one pair of housemartins systematically stealing each blob of mud which their neighbours brought in from the pond, and using them to build their own nest.

I've watched sparrows and blue tits hanging upside down on the red-hot poker flowers, sipping the sweet nectar, and I've been startled to find twenty little yearling newts curled up in the damp coolness beneath a log in the meadow. None of these events are unique or spectacular, but keeping a note of them keeps the experience fresh in my mind, and reminds me of how marvellously rich my wildlife garden is.

These blank pages are for you to fill in in whatever way you fancy – sketches, notes, diagrams – just jot down the dates and wildlife experiences as they happen, and over the years my notebook will become your notebook, and you'll find yourself reading your records over and over again.

Notes

Notes

Notes

Notes

53

Notes

Notes

Notes

Notes

Notes

Notes

Notes

Notes

Native Plants for the Rich – Habitat

(Remember, each of these plants will support its own particular range of dependent insects.)

Trees
Field maple *Acer campestre*
English alder *Alnus glutinosa*
Silver birch *Betula pendula*
Crab apple *Malus sylvestris*
Mountain ash *Sorbus aucuparia*
Wild cherry *Prunus avium*
Hawthorn *Crataegus monogyna*

Shrubs
Alder buckthorn *Frangula alnus*
Hazel *Corylus avellana*
Holly *Ilex aquifolium*
Elder *Sambucus nigra*
Bird cherry *Prunus padus*
Gorse *Ulex europaeus*
Broom *Cytisus scoparius*
Wayfaring tree *Viburnum lantana*
Pussy willow *Salix caprea*
Common buckthorn *Rhamnus catharticus*

Climbers
Honeysuckle *Lonicera periclymenum*
Old man's beard *Clematis vitalba*
Ivy *Hedera helix*

Hedgerow shrubs
Hawthorn *Crataegus monogyna*
Field maple *Acer campestre*
Wild privet *Ligustrum vulgare*
Guelder rose *Viburnum opulus*
Dog rose *Rosa canina*
Blackthorn *Prunus spinosa*
Beech *Fagus sylvatica*
Hornbeam *Carpinus betulus*

WILDFLOWERS

Woodland Edge (or Hedge-Bottom)
Foxglove *Digitalis purpurea*
Primrose *Primula vulgaris*
Yellow archangel *Lamium galeobdolon*
Greater stitchwort *Stellaria holostea*
Greater celandine *Chelidonium majus*
Red campion *Silene dioica*
Red deadnettle *Lamium purpureum*
Hedge mustard *Sisymbrium officinale*
Lily of the valley *Convallaria majalis*
Bluebell *Endymion non-scriptus*
Wood anemone *Anemone nemorosa*
Wood forget-me-not *Myosotis sylvatica*
Snowdrop *Galanthus nivalis*
Violet *Viola riviniana*

Marsh and Pool-Side
Ragged robin *Lychnis flos-cuculi*
Flag iris *Iris pseudacorus*
Flowering rush *Butomus umbellatus*
Purple loose-strife *Lythrum salicaria*
Meadow sweet *Filipendula ulmaria*
Hemp agrimony *Eupatorium cannabinum*
Codlins & cream *Epilobium hirsutum*
Marsh marigold *Caltha palustris*
Greater spearwort *Ranunculus lingua*
Lesser spearwort *Ranunculus flammula*
Water speedwell *Veronica beccabunga*
Marsh birdsfoot trefoil *Lotus uliginosus*
Lesser celandine *Ranunculus ficaria*

Meadow (Spring)
Milkmaids or Lady's smock *Cardamine pratensis*
Cowslip *Primula veris*
Snakehead fritillary *Fritillaria meleagris*
Lesser stitchwort *Stellaria graminea*
Self-heal *Prunella vulgaris*
Bugle *Ajuga reptans*
Daisy *Bellis perennis*
Cat's-ear *Hypochoeris radicata*
Rough hawkbit *Leontodon hispidus*
Dandelion *Taraxacum officinale*

Meadow (Tall Summer)
Knapweed *Centaurea scabiosa*
Lady's bedstraw *Galium verum*
Sheep sorrel *Rumex acetosella*
Field scabious *Knautia arvensis*
Ox-eye daisy *Chrysanthemum leucanthemum*
Hardhead *Centaurea nigra*
Meadow buttercup *Ranunculus acris*

BORDER FLOWERS

Listed in approximate order of flowering –
January to December

Christmas Rose *Helleborus niger*
Winter aconite *Eranthis hyemalis*
Elephant's ears *Bergenia cordifolia*
Spring crocus *Crocus chrysanthus* and
hybrids
Anemone *Anemone blanda*
Grape hyacinth *Muscari botryoides*
Lenten rose *Helleborus orientalis*
Polyanthus *Primula vulgaris elatior*
Soldiers and sailors *Pulmonaria saccharata*
White arabis (single) *Arabis albida*
Honesty *Lunaria biennis*
Sweet Rocket *Hesperis matronalis*
Aubretia *Aubretia deltoides*
Wallflowers *Cheiranthus cheiri*
Forget-me-not *Myosotis* spp
Leopard's-bane *Doronicum pardalianches*
Golden alyssum *Alyssum saxatile*
Sweet William *Dianthus barbatus*
Perennial cornflower *Centaurea*
Poached egg plant *Limnanthes douglasii*
Shasta daisy *Chrysanthemum maximum*
Fleabane *Erigeron speciosus* varieties
Cranesbills *Geranium* species
Sweet bergamot *Monarda didyma*
Evening primrose *Oenothera biennis*
Oriental poppy *Papaver orientale*
Spiked speedwell *Veronica spicata*
Valerian *Centranthus ruber*
Sweet alyssum *Lobularia maritima*
Angelica *Angelica archangelica*
Lovage *Levesticum officinale*
Tobacco plant *Nicotiana alata*
Mignonette *Reseda odorata*
Corncockle *Agrostemma githago*
Yarrow *Achillea filipendulina*
Alkanet *Anchusa azurea*
Chicory *Cichorium intybus*
Yellow loosestrife *Lysimachia vulgaris*
Hollyhock *Alcea rosea*
Snapdragon *Antirrhinum majus*
Candytuft *Iberis umbellata*
Californian poppy *Eschscholzia californica*
Sunflower *Helianthus annuus*
Mallow *Lavatera rosea*
Golden rod *Solidago canadensis*
Phlox *Phlox paniculata*
Teasel *Dipsacus fullonum*
Basil *Ocimum basilicum*
Mint *Mentha rotundifolia*
Globe thistle *Echinops ritro*
Meadow saffron *Colchicum autumnale*
Cosmea *Cosmos bipinnatus*
Cherry pie *Heliotropum x hybridum*
Michaelmas daisy *Aster amellus, A. acris*
          A. novae angliae, A. novi belgii
Ice Plant *Sedum spectabile*

Note: Many of these plants will flower in
autumn if you cut off some of their dead
summer flowers. Don't forget to leave some
to seed.

EXOTIC GARDEN PLANTS

(Service-station plants for wildlife)

Shrubs

Butterfly bush *Buddleia* species
Lilac *Syringa vulgaris* vars.
Snowy mespilus *Amelanchier canadensis*
Barberry *Berberis* species
Californian lilac *Ceanothus (spring
flowering)* spp
Sun rose *Cistus* spp
          Cotoneaster species
          Elaeagnus pungens
          Escallonia hybrids
Lavender *Lavandula spica*
Oregon grape *Mahonia aquifolium*
Mock orange *Philadelphus* varieties
Rosemary *Rosmarinus officinalis*
Shrub roses *Rosa rugosa* & spp
Flowering currant *Ribes sanguineum*
Laurustinus *Viburnum tinus*

Firsts in the Wildlife Garden

Year	19	19	19	19
Snowdrop				
Frogs and spawn				
Primrose				
Butterfly				
Daisy				
Nest-box tenant				
Dragonfly				
Chiff-chaff				
Housemartin				
Swift				
Cuckoo				
Baby bird				
Bat				
Honeysuckle				
Thrush & snail				
Hawk moth				
Spotted flycatcher				
Flying ants				
Hedgehog				
Ripe blackberry				
Redwing				
Fieldfare				
Goldfinch				
Snow				
Bird-table feeding				
Now add your own:				